Angels of Awakening

by Daisy Foss & Laraine Krantz

To Heidi

May the Angels
always be with
you xxx

love Daisy Foss

Universal Lessons of Love, Life & Creation

Daisy 'Raine

First published by Daisy 'Raine MMVI

Angels of Awakening ~ Universal Lessons of Love,
Life & Creation: First published by Daisy 'Raine 2006

Angels of Awakening ~ Universal Lessons of Love,
Life & Creation written by Daisy Foss©

Angels of Awakening ~ Universal Lessons of Love,
Life & Creation photographed by Laraine Krantz©

Artwork: www.picagraphicltd.com
Printed and bound by www.westdale.co.uk

Available from www.daisycentres.com

ISBN-10: 0-9553701-0-8
ISBN-13: 978-0-9553701-0-6

A dedication to Angels everywhere

We wish to thank, bless and praise everyone
we have met on our path who has helped
us to bring these lessons to you.

We have loved every moment working with
them and wish for you to feel this love too.

We hope we have "Awakened the Angel"
in all of you.

Contents

Universal Lessons of Love, Life & Creation

Universal Lessons of Love

Contents continued...

Universal Lessons of Life

Universal Lessons of Creation

Angels of Awakening
Universal Lessons of Love, Life & Creation
An Introduction

We have invited the Angels of Awakening to teach us the basics of these Laws of the Universe, exploring the Lessons of Love, Life and Creation. These Angelic stone statues symbolise the ancient longevity, the silent grace, and great wisdom of these Angels. Such stone statues are all around us, as monuments, as decorations on buildings, as guardians of our loved ones and in our homes as gifts. The Angels of Awakening breathe love and create new understanding ~ they bring to life the Lessons of Love, Life and Creation for all those who wish to experience them.

Whenever our issues overwhelm or confuse us the Angels of Awakening help us to find our way and to open ourselves to the love and the joy that is ours by divine right. Angels are messengers from God, the source of unconditional love of the Universe. As omnipresent beings they lead us across bridges of hope and faith. As we learn our Lessons of Life, they assist us to fully experience our existence, to achieve our Divine Purpose and to recognise our unique gifts. As we awaken to our spiritual truth the Angels become more obvious in our lives.

These Lessons will help us to understand and develop a deep sense of well being and unconditional love. There are many interpretations of the Universal Laws of Life. We have chosen 36, which will be a guide for spiritual awakening and enlightenment. Take time to be silent and meditate on how best these Lessons of Love, Life and Creation can help to give you a better understanding of the difficulties or challenges you may be experiencing in daily life.

These are Spiritual Laws. They are the Laws of the Universe that we all live by, whether we are conscious of them or not. For most people Laws usually mean rules and control over the masses. The Lessons within these Laws empower us. They are Lessons of Love, Life and Creation. "Love is all there is" to affirm the source of the divine in all of us. "Life" is the journey we all undertake to gain experience of ourselves in this realm. "Creation" is the manifestation of all that is, the outcome of cause and effect.

The 36 Lessons of Life are also known as Laws of the Universe or the Universal Spiritual Laws of Nature. Divine Source is the basis of Human nature, living in harmony with the other realms of existence. A Lesson can be fun and we can gain great knowledge from it. It can be a hard lesson forced upon us, a Lesson we will never forget or the Lessons may be the same ones over and over again providing a pattern of experience to learn from gradually. These Lessons have been handed down through our human behaviour patterns. Some of us have learnt them early and easily; others have struggled with them or stumbled upon them later in life. Just by knowing the laws and the natural flow that connects us all on every level of existence, call to the Angels and be active with the intention to find strength and wisdom as you learn from Life.

The way we live has moved on dramatically yet the Lessons of Love, Life and Creation have hardly changed at all, they have easily adjusted to our modern times. As time seems to go faster we can experience anger, fear, unforgiveness, anxiety and stress of any kind resulting in dis-ease, depression, even life threatening long term illness. Daily life used to be at a much slower pace, it took months to travel around the world. We can now achieve many of the opportunities our ancestors only ever dreamed of. These are our reality and we take many of these miracles for granted.

Know that these Laws are not man-made but gifted from the Universal Source of Love. As we go within our hearts, we discover our inner wisdom an abundance of faith, hope and truth in all things. A heavy heart feels full of despair, loneliness and unhappiness. Our body might feel filled with anger, hate and bitterness. To achieve a light heart, we ask the Angels to help us to feel it brimming and overflowing with love, joy, forgiveness and peace as the Love and Angelic Light radiates through every cell in our body.

Be a Human Being not a Human Doing. Embrace this state of being, living these lessons to the best of our abilities we will experience abundance of joy, happiness, peace and serenity. The glow of acceptance will shine through the Lessons of Love, Life and Creation fully on a daily basis ~ Blessed be the Angels of Awakening.

How to Awaken to these Angels

The Lessons of Love, Life and Creation in this book can be accessed in many ways. Find a quiet space for contemplation, light a candle, hold a crystal and invite the Angels of Awakening to join you. We suggest you have a special journal to record your innermost thoughts as you continue on this journey of discovery and understanding of the most important person in your life ~ you.

Reflect on every lesson either with a group of friends, or by yourself. When you connect to your Divine Essence Self you will find your truth in any situation. You will be able to link with your Angels to obtain a better understanding of how and why things manifest in your life the way they do.

You may read this Lessons of Love, Life and Creation book from front cover to back cover or you may dip into it, choosing an image using the synchronicity and guidance of the Angels. There is no right or wrong way to receive a message from the Angels of Awakening. Be organic and follow your heart and read these however you feel in the moment.

By embracing the fundamental lessons of Love, Life and Creation you will experience a happy, contented and peaceful existence that you can share with others.

~ The Angels invite you to be awakened with your Angelic Light

Universal Lessons of Love, Life & Creation

Universal Lessons of Love

The Lesson of Unconditional Love

Love without conditions or strings
attached is pure love.

See the beauty, light and divinity
in every living thing all around.

Do not expect something in return before
you give your love and affection ~ release
any grudges or unforgiveness to the Angels.

Be free from judgement against anyone
or any situation ~ then you are able
to receive unconditional love with no
demands, expectations or judgements.

Radiate the essence of love, joy and compassion
through every moment, action & desire.

The greatest gift is the power of love ~
not the love of power ~ love conquers all.

Universal Lessons of Love

The Lesson of Grace

Grace is a state of being, serenity and calm
in your pure beauty.

The consequences of Karma are released
through divine grace, when you connect
to a higher vibration.

Be graceful in all your actions, thoughts
and deeds. With a deep understanding
of how you react and control your emotions,
be balanced, calm and relaxed.

Maintain the inner poise of love and
understanding; treat others how you
would wish to be cared for.
Bring in divine grace.

Unconditionally love yourself and all others.
Be gracious in your manner.

Universal Lessons of Love

The Lesson of Self Love

Love yourself unconditionally with every cell,
atom and electron of your body. Feel love
in every thought and deed.

By loving yourself you radiate the vibration
to feel the warmth and emotion of true love.

Be kind and considerate to yourself when
you feel fear, anger and unforgiveness arise.
Release these negative issues to the Angels ~
take care of yourself.

Treat yourself with respect and compassion ~
love who you are.

Have the courage to show love for yourself
in everything you say and do.

The Lesson of Forgiveness

Forgiveness is born of unconditional love.

Be able to understand another's point of view
without condemnation. Recognise their right
to free will and their belief systems.

To be able to forgive and forget is truly
a compassionate act. Holding on to the past
hurt and resentment only prolongs the agony.

Release all judgement and really
demonstrate your forgiving nature with
strength and sincerity. Do not hold on
to the pain or bear grudges.

There is no fear in forgiving, only
"for giving" of your unconditional love.

Universal Lessons of Love

The Lesson of Free Will

Free will is the divine choice to be who you truly are. This is a gift for you to create your own reality, to choose every moment in your life.

Use your will positively to enhance your spiritual growth and divine plan. Be loving and responsible in your thoughts and actions.

Reclaim your power, behold your free will and express your joy. Do not allow others to control your being by giving away your power. Release all fear.

Experience every moment, go with the flow, and choose your spiritual growth.

The Lesson of Compassion

Compassion is unconditional love,
made manifest.

In every thought and action feel yourself
compassionately compounding the love,
expanding it out to bring joy and happiness
through the Universe.

Feel the other person's point of view, be open
to sharing and giving without reward, release
any judgement to the Angels.

Open your heart with a deep gracious
willingness to help, in whatever way
you are able.

Feel the strength of compassion, the peace
and the wisdom that it brings you.

Universal Lessons of Love

The Lesson of Faith

Believe, trust and have faith in yourself.

Faith is a feeling, a system of belief,
a conviction upheld.

Know there is a grand plan, a Divine Purpose.
Surrender the fear, anger, and release these
emotions ~ keep your faith and trust safe
in your loving heart.

Expand your awareness, have faith
in immeasurable love ~ be confident
in your aspiration and loyalties.

Believe without proof, and surrender
to your knowing.

Universal Lessons of Life

The Lesson of Acceptance

Accept others as you wish to be treated,
with love and understanding.

Resist the temptation to interfere in other's
decisions and life choices ~ refrain from
trying to control situations.

Surrender and accept the free will of your
loved ones. Support them with wise words
of experience ~ then allow them to walk
their own path.

Angels do not judge, they accept you
unconditionally. Judge not, for if you do,
you will be judged.

Accept responsibility for your actions
and allow others to sing their own song.

Universal Lessons of Love

The Lesson of Hope

Hope is the feeling inside of knowing all
is safe and secure, a positive affirmation
of trust and faith.

Without hope, there is despair and a sense
of abandonment. When you have hope,
there is a silent strong feeling supporting
your spiritual awareness.

Negative fears can destroy any hope in
a situation. Believe in a positive outcome
by connecting to your Angels and overcome
any difficulties or problems.

When you have dreams and aspirations,
it is hope that brings them alive.
Have faith in yourself and your future.

Wherever there is hope there is life,
Wherever there is life there is hope.

Universal Lessons of Love

The Lesson of Patience

Patience is surrendering to the serenity of
the moment, being relaxed, calm and content.

Have a divine knowing, an understanding
of the bigger picture, a patient disposition
allowing life to unfold gracefully.

Trust that everything in nature has
divine timing and release the need to
control, to be frustrated and impatient
for things to manifest.

Find the stillness in your open heart
to portray a sense of unconditional
love and acceptance.

Patience is a virtue gifted by the Angels.

Universal Lessons of Love

The Lesson of Joy

Joy is an expression of peace and happiness.

A joyful attitude brings a special spontaneity
and purpose to you and your loved ones.

An overwhelming feeling of deep happiness
and excitement ~ this is the experience of joy.

As you open your heart to the wonders
of this world, you can express this emotion
of unconditional love with a smile,
a song or a dance.

Find the pure love and joy in your life
with trust and faith in the Angels.

Universal Lessons of Love

The Lesson of Praise

Show your appreciation, love
and gratitude with praise.

Praise every thing and every one
in your life for every achievement
in every beautiful moment.

Refrain from criticising, or being negative,
recognise the effort and build confidence
with motivation, thanks and honest praise.

Give praise and receive it for all your efforts
and blessings. Praise given from a joyful
heart sends ripples through your being.

Be slow to judge, but quick to praise.

Universal Lessons of Love

The Lesson of Oneness

We are all equal in Divine Oneness.

The Divine source is infinite. In separation, we feel fear when we feel alone.

When we experience oneness, our soul grows and the Universe flows through us.

By sharing our talents, we are transmuting the energy to a higher vibration and helping planetary ascension.

Teach others to understand we are one ~ we are all there is.

The Lesson of Action

Every action produces a reaction.

Actions spring from an idea, a thought visualised and carried out with intention.

Healing thoughts bring peace and understanding ~ healing action produces well-being.

Create your reality, your Divine Purpose. Put into action your ideas and manifest your world.

Actions speak louder than words.

The Lesson of Creativity

Be creative and unique in everything
you do ~ every moment of the day.

Every single soul is creating their reality
every moment of the day. We all co-create
the environment we live in.

Be creative in recognising your desires,
thoughts and actions. All your talent
and unique qualities can produce beauty
and Love in your Life.

Be true to your feelings and create
a lifestyle that is yours by Divine Right
in a positive and loving way.

Creativity is the gift of "being you"
in your divine power.

Universal Lessons of Life

The Lesson of Attraction

As magnetic beings, we attract the
vibration we radiate.

We create our environment, our lives, by the
thoughts and desires of our dreams, then we
manifest them into our lives.

Harness the lesson of attraction by creating the
Life you want in a positive and loving way.

Think beautiful positive thoughts, aspirations,
and you will attract them to yourself.

Be negative and blocked in an ego position
and you will attract the ego pattern and
conditioning that goes with it.

Give Love, compassion and a smile ~
and attract Love, compassion and a smile.

Universal Lessons of Life

The Lesson of Cause & Effect

Every thought causes an effect
and every effect has a cause.

When thoughts of anger, fear or resentment
are out of control in your mind, you project
these misqualified energies, harming
yourself and others.

We call the principle of cause and effect
Karma ~ what goes around comes around.

It is the same for everyone and manifests
through physical actions and thoughts.

Think Love ~ feel Love and you will attract Love.

Universal Lessons of Life

The Lesson of Responsibility

Only you can be responsible for
your hopes and dreams.

Be positive and in touch with all your
hopes, aspirations and expectations.

Take control of your responsibilities.
Establish your boundaries and duties
by being honest and true to yourself
on your journey.

Release any burdens you carry of blame,
fear or denial of your responsibilities.

Be responsible for your own thoughts,
actions and experiences.

Universal Lessons of Life

The Lesson of Honesty

Be responsible for how honest you feel.
Be understanding, patient and loving to
yourself and all others.

By ignoring your inner guidance and
lying to yourself, the only one being
harmed is you.

How honest are you being with yourself?
Ask yourself how true to your feelings
you act.

Come to the answers of life's quandaries
by honestly evaluating how you feel ~ does
your heart sing or your stomach flutter?

Be kind to yourself ~ ask your heart
which direction will honestly benefit
your divine life purpose plan.

Universal Lessons of Life

The Lesson of Motion

Every thought is pure energy,
movement from the Source.

Energy is found in many forms ~
it can always be transformed but never
created or destroyed.

Atoms in our bodies, minds and all
things around us vibrate at different
levels ~ they are in constant motion.

Movement is continuous ~ your heart
beats, your breath flows, your loving
thoughts create your world.

Be conscious of your thoughts and
actions as they move from one state
to another.

Universal Lessons of Life

The Lesson of Polarity

Polarity is the balance of all things.

When things are poles apart they seem unconnected, separated by time and space ~ they are however 'one'.

To experience sound, you must know silence. The knowledge of hot and cold also reveals warmth, the compromise, the middle.

Choose from the extremes of love and hate, dark and light with a balanced understanding of love, trust and faith.

As above, so below ~ as within, so without.

Universal Lessons of Life

The Lesson of Energy

Energy is every thought, desire and action.

We are all a mass of molecules
moving energetically.

Our physical bodies are the densest, followed
by our etheric bodies all vibrating at different
speeds, making up our energy bodies.

Energy is the Source. It changes and
transmutes as it moves through
alternative vibrations.

There is always movement in energy.
It is never lost ~ it just changes from
one form to another.

Universal Lessons of Life

The Lesson of Rhythm

Everything in the Universe moves with
a natural rhythm.

Mother Nature is in harmony and
balance, and dependant on rhythm.

When we are at peace with ourselves and
in harmony with our surroundings, we
must listen and respect the rhythm of
the Universe.

The waters rise and fall ~ the days and
nights come and go in perfect harmony
and rhythm.

Your heart beats, your blood flows.
Find your own rhythm and balance ~
be in tune with your body.

Life itself goes with the flow ~
go with the flow of Love in your Life.

Universal Lessons of Life

54

The Lesson of Relativity

Know your own reality ~
trust that every situation is relative.

Relativity is the experience of measuring
things in relation to each other.

By comparing your past knowledge
of fear and unhappiness, you can feel
the difference when you choose
positive qualities of Love and joy.

Without relationship, there is no wisdom
or history, so bless these in your life and
seek a relative answer to your prayers.

All things are relative.

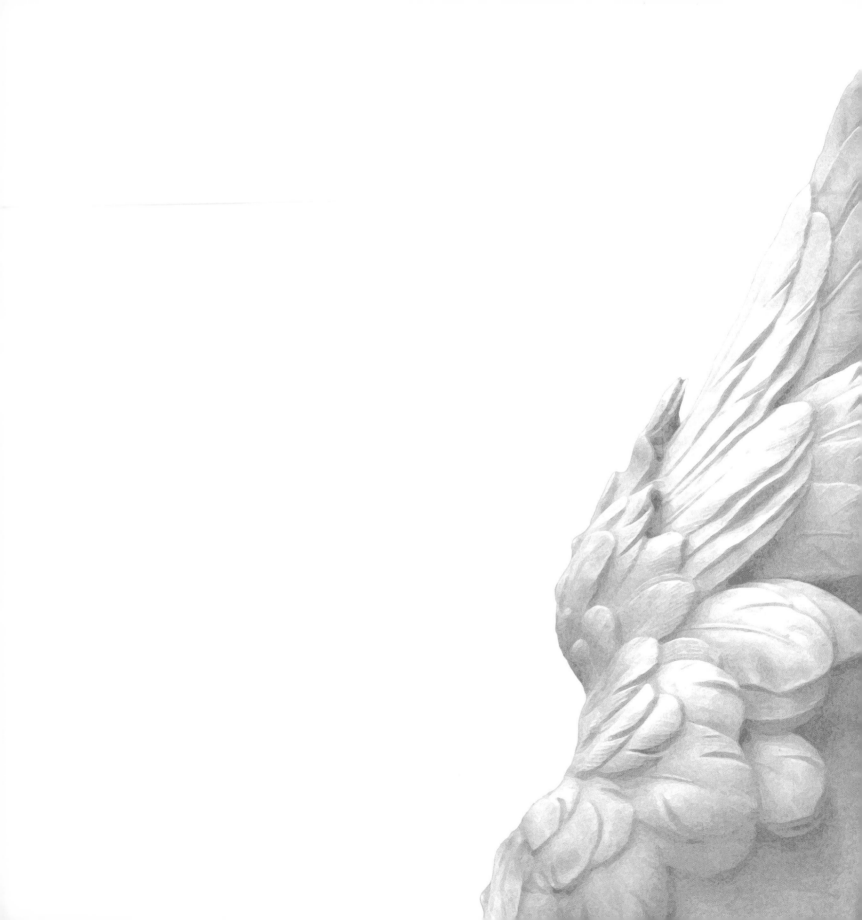

Universal Lessons of Creation

The Lesson of Kindness

Kindness is an act of unconditional love.

A random act of kindness swells the heart
and brings a smile, joy and happiness.

Show kindness in many ways ~
it costs you nothing.

Never feel or be superior ~ this is the
ego being judgemental.

Give from your generous heart,
and let others see your example.

Treat others as kindly as you wish
to be treated.

Universal Lessons of Creation

The Lesson of Compensation

Compensation is a reward from the Angels ~
a gift from the Divine for every loving
thought and action you take.

Shower your love unconditionally ~
use your talents wisely and you will
receive priceless compensation.

Give fully from an open heart full of joy
and compassion, and the Universe will
return this love to you in abundance
when you least expect it.

When you give unconditionally
without an expected outcome ~
you will be rewarded ten fold.

Be open to giving and receiving Angelic Love.

Universal Lessons of Creation

The Lesson of Charity

Charity is an openhearted gesture of kindness ~ sharing what you have.

Be generous with your gifts to keep the flow of energy. Never judge others and always be positive in your outlook.

Charity begins at home and spreads throughout the Universe.

Taking responsibility for your actions by helping others is an act of charity.

Giving unconditionally from your heart to those less fortunate than you, with compassion is charity.

The Lesson of Aspiration

Be an inspiration to yourself
and others at all times.

Aspire to the best of your abilities
by using your gifts in the most
courageously loving way.

Dream of your aspirations and
expectations ~ believe in yourself and
achieve your goals.

Be fully connected to your Angelic Realm
~ by being happy, joyful and loving,

Aspire to radiate love, joy and compassion
in all areas of your life.

Universal Lessons of Creation

The Lesson of Courage

Courage is the strength of character
to stand up for your beliefs.

The courage of your conviction is to be
focused on what you believe and feel in your
heart, and then to act upon it.

When you feel weak and overwhelmed,
ask for guidance and courage to go forward
with pride and strength in everything
you think, say and do.

Have the courage to be honest and
true to your thoughts and to learn
from your experiences.

Never fear. Be strong and positive ~
trust that all is safe and secure.

Universal Lessons of Creation

68

The Lesson of Generosity

Give with a loving, open, heartfelt
gesture of generosity.

Be generous by sharing your wealth,
wisdom, your gifts, and your time
with no fear or other agenda.

Do not be attached to things, people
or places ~ give lovingly and share
your gifts freely.

Generosity is a knowing of being
abundant ~ it is a manifestation of
unconditional Love.

What goes around comes around ~
as you give so you will receive.

Universal Lessons of Creation

The Lesson of Dedication

Dedication is being committed
one hundred percent.

Trust that you know what you have
dedicated yourself to is honest and
right for you on all levels.

Be sure that you check out your feelings
fully before you dive right into a situation
or cause ~ ask for guidance and review
your progress regularly.

Think about the effect of your actions ~
trust your inner intuition, and be
dedicated to your faith in yourself.

Be true to yourself when you dedicate
your Life to your Divine Purpose.

Universal Lessons of Creation

The Lesson of Thankfulness

Be thankful for all your gifts,
wisdom and happiness.

Appreciate everyone and every thing in your
life ~ be glad, and count your blessings.

Never take anyone or anything for granted ~
make each thought one of praise and thanks.

Have a positive and loving outlook in your
life ~ be grateful for all your experiences.

Have the attitude of gratitude.

Universal Lessons of Creation

The Lesson of Abundance

Abundance consciousness is a state of being.

Have faith in the knowledge that all will
be provided for you, as love and money
moves freely through your life.

Give without fear, criticism or judgements.
Know the abundance will be shared with you ~
go with the law of least resistance.

When you feel safe, content and wealthy
in a spiritual sense you will want for nothing ~
you know the Angels will supply
everything you desire.

Abundance is trusting in the Universal flow.

Universal Lessons of Creation

The Lesson of Gender

Balance is the key to the law of gender.

The qualities of the male and the female are both positive and negative, good or bad, light or dark ~ it depends on your point of view.

Each situation depends on the circumstances ~ intention is all that matters. How masculine is the man or feminine is the woman?

Respect the part of you that is striving for balance.

Recognise the love and truth of the entwined male and female parts of yourself and all others.

Universal Lessons of Creation

78

The Lesson of Leadership

Leadership is an action that demonstrates your commitment.

Trust, integrity and honesty are qualities most sought after in a leader, and are generally recognised as such.

Are you are a spiritual leader or a follower?

Be willing to share the knowledge and wisdom you have gathered. Offer it to others and be fearless in your belief in their truth. Refrain from bullying ~ do not dictate your wishes.

Often in times of challenge, the one who is strongest or cleverest takes the lead, to define a position or to win a battle for the good of all.

A leader is born with the gift of showing the way forward by example.

Universal Lessons of Creation

The Lesson of Correspondence

Correspondence is balance through
Universal connection.

Everything throughout the Universe is
connected, no sound without silence,
no light without dark, no up without down.

The butterfly flaps its wings on one side of the
world and we have a storm on the other side.
Nothing is isolated or alone in this world ~
we all affect each other in some way.

The mind, body and spirit all correspond
to health, harmony and balance ~
for every action, there is a reaction.

Be connected within and you shall be
connected without.

Universal Lessons of Creation